A CAT NAMED CLYDE

A CAT NAMED CLYDE

A TIMELESS TALE *of* NATURAL CHANGES

told by

ELLEN SHELTON

illustrated by

BARBARA HUDIN

WESTERN EYE PRESS
2016

This is the story of a cat named Clyde
who had lots of adventures…after he died.

Oh, it might seem to you that he just disappeared
if you looked in his meadow grave after a year,

but nothing can "just disappear," you should know,
it only can change, though it might not show

to a person who doesn't know quite where to look.
And that's what you'll find out by reading this book.…

Clyde had been buried for a week, maybe two,

when he felt something different. He felt something new.

His trusty cat spirit was there, still intact,

but his body was changing. And that was a fact!

Part of Clyde turned into dirt

where flowers grew. It didn't hurt.

It felt, instead, rather grand,

this transformation into land.

For the tall thin grasses that Clyde the cat grew

were the very same ones he used to stalk through.

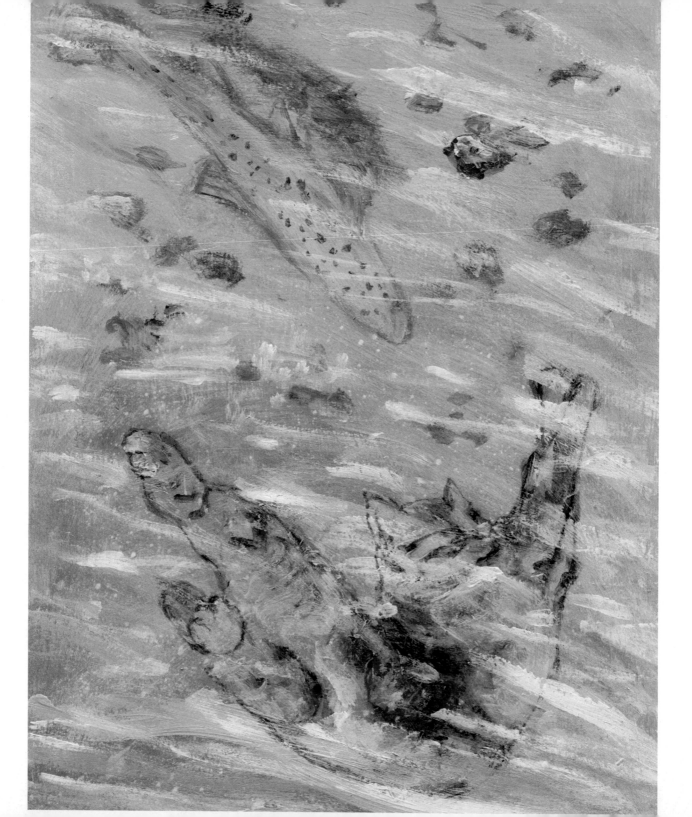

And some of Clyde went all the way down

to a stream that was flowing deep under the ground.

He then joined a river on its way to an ocean

and there found himself in perpetual motion.

.

He found himself, too, on very hot days
being changed into mist and made into haze.

He was lifted quite gently by the warmth of the sun
up into the sky. He thought it was fun.

And while Clyde was part of the sky, as a cloud,
he sailed close to sunsets and felt rather proud

of the way that his color and shape would change
as he drifted across each dark mountain range.

But clouds can't stay clouds for a very long time,
so neither could Clyde continue to climb

on currents of air and drift without aim.
One day he just had to turn into rain.

Well, we know it rained cats, and it might have rained dogs,
because the stream in Clyde's meadow swept rocks and big logs

away in a flood of meadow debris.
And it all ended up, once again, at the sea.

One of Clyde's rocks ended up on a beach
where it lay many years just within reach

of the waves which turned it into fine sand,
a grain of which just happened to land

on an oyster who opened his shell for a minute.
And the next thing he knew, Clyde was there in it

Well, that oyster made Clyde into a pearl
that was worn by a woman who liked to twirl

her strand of white beads around and around.
(This made Clyde wish he were back in the ground!)

Meanwhile in the meadow where this story began,
a pine tree was growing. It had quite a span.

"Just right," thought a woodsman who saw it one day.
So he cut it down and took it away.

Of course part of Clyde was there in that tree,
the very best part, it could well be.

For the wood became both heat and light
as Clyde's tree burned throughout the night,

warming the house of that old woodsman
and his nine grey cats. Or was it ten?

It's not at all easy to keep track of Clyde
who's become so much more than a cat who had died.

A cat whose time might just have ended
except for the other times he was intended

to give all of what had made him a cat
to things that were quite a bit different than that.

So, Clyde's still around, though a cat he is not.
He'll always be something, somewhere, and somewhat.

THE AUTHORS

Ellen Shelton has lived with, and said goodbye to a number of family pets. And she has thought long and lovingly of the journey that their essence, their substance and their spirit, then make in this natural world. The idea of transformation comforted her young daughters, and she hopes that the story of Clyde may help other children see the death of a pet as not quite so final. Ellen lives in Bend, Oregon, with her writer husband Peter.

Barbara Hudin also lives, and paints, in Bend, Oregon. Her paintings can be seen at the Tumalo Art Co. gallery in Bend.

A Cat Named Clyde is their first collaboration.

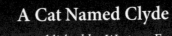

A Cat Named Clyde

is published by Western Eye Press,
a small independent press
(very small and very independent)
with a home base in
the Colorado Rockies
and an office
in Sedona Arizona.

text © 2016 Ellen Shelton
illustrations © 2016 Barbara Hudin
Western Eye Press
PO Box 1008
Sedona AZ 86339
1 800 333 5178
www.WesternEyePress.com
ISBN13: 978-0-941283-44-1

Made in the USA
San Bernardino, CA
25 October 2016